Welcome to
LIBERIA

Gareth Stevens Publishing
A WORLD ALMANAC EDUCATION GROUP COMPANY

Written by
YUMI NG

Edited by
MELVIN NEO

Edited in USA by
JENETTE DONOVAN GUNTLY

Designed by
GEOSLYN LIM

Picture research by
SUSAN JANE MANUEL

First published in North America in 2005 by
Gareth Stevens Publishing
A World Almanac Education Group Company
330 West Olive Street, Suite 100
Milwaukee, Wisconsin 53212 USA

Please visit our web site at
www.garethstevens.com
For a free color catalog describing
Gareth Stevens Publishing's list of high-quality
books and multimedia programs,
call 1-800-542-2595 (USA) or
1-800-387-3178 (Canada).
Gareth Stevens Publishing's fax: (414) 332-3567.

© **MARSHALL CAVENDISH INTERNATIONAL (ASIA)
PRIVATE LIMITED 2004**
Originated and designed by
Times Editions Marshall Cavendish
An imprint of Marshall Cavendish International (Asia) Pte Ltd
A member of Times Publishing Limited
Times Centre, 1 New Industrial Road
Singapore 536196
http://www.timesone.com.sg/te

Library of Congress Cataloging-in-Publication Data
Ng, Yumi.
Welcome to Liberia / by Yumi Ng.
p. cm. — (Welcome to my country)
Includes bibliographical references and index.
ISBN 0-8368-2566-7 (lib. bdg.)
1. Liberia — Juvenile literature. I. Title. II. Series.
DT624.N44   2004
966.62—dc22   2004042877

Printed in Singapore

1 2 3 4 5 6 7 8 9 08 07 06 05 04

PICTURE CREDITS
Agence France Presse: 13, 37
Bettmann/Corbis: 10
Camera Press Ltd: 39
Getty Images/Hulton Archive: 11, 12, 14,
    15 (bottom), 23, 26
iAfrika: 4, 18, 20 (left and right), 21, 27, 43
Bernt Karlsson: 29, 38, 45
Martin Klejnowski Kennedy: 17, 22
Karen E. Lange: 3 (center), 7, 8, 16 (bottom),
    24, 34, 36, 40, 41
Lonely Planet Images: 33 (top)
Dawn Padmore: 30
Panos Pictures: cover, 16 (top)
Philadelphia Zoo: 15 (top)
Albrecht G. Schaefer/Corbis: 6, 9
Liba Taylor: 28, 32
Still Pictures: 1, 5, 25, 31, 35
Topham Picturepoint: 2, 3 (top), 19
Werner Forman Archive: 3 (bottom),
    33 (bottom left and right)

Digital Scanning by Superskill Graphics Pte Ltd

Contents

Words that appear in the glossary are printed in **boldface** type the first time they occur in the text.

Welcome to Liberia!

Liberia is the oldest **republic** in Africa. It was founded by a group of African Americans in 1847. Liberia has many natural resources and could become a wealthy nation, but years of civil war have kept the country from growing. Let's explore Liberia and learn about its interesting people!

Opposite: Because of Liberia's civil war, soldiers from the Community of West African States were sent in to help keep the peace.

Below: These Liberian children are raising their country's flag with pride.

The Flag of Liberia

The flag of Liberia has red and white stripes and a blue square box at the top left corner. The white star stands for Liberia, which was Africa's first republic. The colors red, white, and blue represent courage, purity, and loyalty.

The Land

Liberia is located on the west coast of Africa. Its area is about 43,000 square miles (111,370 square kilometers). The country is surrounded by land on three sides and the Atlantic Ocean to the southwest. Liberia is divided into four regions: coastal plains, rolling hills, low mountains, and northern highlands. The coastal plains contain beaches, **lagoons**, swamps, forests, and farms.

Below: This beach in Monrovia, the capital city, is a popular tourist spot.

The second region contains many lush green hills. Cocoa and coffee are often grown in the hills region. The third region contains low mountains that are up to 1,000 feet (305 meters) tall. The region also has **savannas**. The fourth region, the northern highlands, is located near Liberia's border with Guinea. The country's highest peak, Mount Wuteve, or Wutivi, is located in the northern highlands. The peak is 4,528 feet (1,380 m) high. The country also has many large rivers, including the Mano, Morro, and Cavalla Rivers.

Climate

Liberia's climate varies with the land's height above sea level. The coastal plains are low. For most of the year, the weather there is damp, with average temperatures of about 80° Fahrenheit (27° Celsius). The high inland regions are cooler and drier. In the northern highlands, the average temperature is about 65° F (18° C). The country has two seasons. The dry season is from November to April. The rainy season is from May to October. During the rainy season, some regions get as much as 205 inches (5,207 millimeters) of rain.

Left: During the rainy season, many of Liberia's rivers overflow and turn roads into pits of mud. Flooding is an especially big problem in the inland regions.

Plants and Animals

Liberia's forests contain many types of trees, including teak, ebony, and rubber trees. The country is also home to many animals, including crocodiles, pygmy hippopotamuses, and manatees. The white-shouldered duiker, a kind of deer, and the zebra antelope are **native** to the country. Birds such as the lesser kestrel and the Liberia greenbul live in the rain forests. Many of the country's plants and animals are **endangered** because of the destruction of Liberia's rain forests.

History

African groups such as the Mande and the Kru were some of the first people to live in what is now Liberia. They most likely came from northeastern Africa in the 1100s A.D. The groups lived by hunting and farming. By the mid-1200s, they had begun to trade slaves, gold, and other items with northern Africans.

In 1461, a Portuguese sailor named Pedro de Sintra came to Liberia. Later, more Europeans came to trade for gold, palm oil, and a very valuable spice that was known as Melegueta pepper.

Left:
This illustration shows an artist's impression of an early **settlement** in what is now Liberia. At that time, the region was called the Guinea Coast.

From the 1600s to the 1800s, the main trade between the Africans and the Europeans was in slaves.

The Colony of Liberia

In 1816, the American Colonization Society was founded. The aim of the group was to send freed slaves and freeborn African Americans to Africa to form a **colony**. The first colony was established by the early 1820s. More were built later. In 1847, many of them joined to form the Republic of Liberia.

An Unequal Society

The African Americans who settled in Liberia were called Americo-Liberians. When the Americo-Liberians created their laws, they did not give equal rights to the native people. The native people were still forced to pay taxes and work for the Americo-Liberians in conditions almost like slavery, but they were not given the same rights. As a result, the native people often fought back. The small fights turned into larger battles in 1822, 1856, and 1875.

Left: This drawing shows an artist's impression of the 1839 **mutiny** aboard the *Amistad*, a slave ship that carried many slaves taken from Liberia. Some of Liberia's colonial settlers were former slaves rescued from illegal slave ships like the *Amistad*.

Left: Throughout the 1980s, fighting continued on the streets of Monrovia, Liberia's capital city, and elsewhere. Many Liberians were unhappy with the leadership of Samuel Doe and with the economy.

The Twentieth Century

The Americo-Liberians formed only a small part of the population of Liberia, but they had control of the government and industry. In 1944, William Tubman became president. He worked hard to help native Liberians get more rights.

In the 1970s, the economy worsened. Many citizens blamed the government. In 1980, President William Tolbert was killed in a violent **coup** led by Master Sergeant Samuel Kanyon Doe.

The Civil war (1989–1996)

Samuel Doe was elected president in 1985. Doe's government was violent and dishonest and made the economy worse. In 1989, a civil war broke out between the government and **rebels** led by Charles Ghankay Taylor. Liberia's African neighbors sent soldiers to keep peace in the country. In 1990, the rebels killed President Doe. The war finally ended in 1996. In 1997, Charles Taylor became president. The fighting started again in 2000. To keep peace, Taylor was **exiled** to Nigeria in 2003.

Left:
Liberian rebels stand at attention outside their camp in August 1992.

Alexander Peal (1945–)

Alexander Peal played on Liberia's national soccer team and later used his fame to promote his **environmental** work. He helped set up the country's only national park. In 2000, he won the Goldman Environmental Prize.

Alexander Peal

Samuel Kanyon Doe (c. 1950–1990)

Samuel Doe joined the army at age eighteen. A native Liberian, he was unhappy with the Americo-Liberian government. Doe led a successful coup in 1980. He became Liberia's first native Liberian president.

Charles Ghankay Taylor (1948–)

Charles Taylor served under President Doe but was forced to flee to the United States when he was accused of being dishonest. He later returned. In 1997, he became president. In 2003, Taylor was exiled after being charged with helping rebels in several West African nations.

Charles Taylor

Government and the Economy

The Americo-Liberians created a political party called the True Whig Party, which ruled Liberia from 1878 to 1980. The party gave many rights to Americo-Liberians but overlooked the needs of native Liberians. The party fell apart when Samuel Doe, who was a native Liberian, took over in 1980. A new **constitution** was adopted in 1986 that allows different political parties to take part in the country's elections.

Above: Liberia's national **emblem** was based on the emblem of the United States.

Left: This woman voted in Liberia's 1997 presidential elections.

The government of Liberia has three branches. The legislative branch makes laws and collect taxes. It is made up of the House of Representatives and the Senate. The president is the head of the executive branch and the government. The president serves a six-year term and is in charge of choosing ministers for the cabinet. The ministers serve as the president's advisers. The judiciary branch includes a Supreme Court and a system of lower courts.

Above: In 1998, these Liberian boys stood in front of what used to be the Ministry of Internal Affairs. It was used as a shelter during the civil war. Many parts of Liberia's government did not always function during the long war, including the judiciary branch.

The Economy

Liberia's long civil war has hurt the economy. In the 1990s, the country's main source of income, farming, was almost shut down because so many farmers joined the military, were forced off their farms, or were killed. Liberia's farmers have now returned to work, but the farms are not producing as much as they did before the war. The country's main farm products are rice, sugarcane, cocoa, coffee, palm oil, and **cassava**.

Left: Since the end of Liberia's civil war, farmers have once again begun to plant new crops, including vegetable crops like this one.

Rubber and Mining

Other important Liberian industries include rubber producing and mining. Rubber is a major Liberian **export**, but the industry has not yet recovered from the war. Mining is also an important industry. **Iron ore** was once Liberia's main mining product, but the mines have now run out of iron, and no new mines have been dug. Today, miners focus on mining gold and diamonds.

Above: A cargo ship from Liberia transports goods to a port in Georgia in the United States. In 2000, Liberia sold most of its exports to the United States, Belgium, Germany, and Italy.

People and Lifestyle

More than three million people live in
Liberia. About 95 percent of them are
native Africans. They come from many
ethnic groups, including the Kpelle,
Bassa, Gio, Krahn, Kru, Mano, Grebo,
Gola, Loma, Gbandi, Kissi, Vai, and
Bella groups. Less than 3 percent of
Liberians are Americo-Liberians.

Below, left:
Liberian women
give birth to an
average of about
six children each.

Below, right: In
Liberia, elderly
people are highly
respected. They
often serve as
judges and leaders
in their villages.

City and Country Life

About 40 percent of Liberians live in
the large cities of Monrovia, Buchanan,
Harper, and Greenville. **Urban** people
work in many different kinds of jobs.
They usually live in buildings made of
permanent materials, such as cement.
The rest of Liberia's population live in
the countryside. They most often work
as farmers, but some work as traders,
artists, or hunters. Most **rural** people
live in less sturdy buildings, such as
huts or simple wooden homes.

Family Life

Liberian families are usually very close. Often, many family members live in the same house or area. In some native Liberian communities, a group for men called the *Poro* (POH-roh), and one for women, called the *Sande* (SAHN-day), play an important role in society. These groups teach men and women proper behavior. They also teach traditional ways of life and native religion.

Below: As a result of the civil war, this Liberian family fled to the country of Ghana, where they lived in a **refugee** camp. In 1998, they were forced to go back to Liberia.

Liberian Women

Most Liberian women marry under traditional Liberian law. They do not have the right to keep their children or to **inherit** property if their husbands die. Under Liberia's civil law, women have more rights, but the laws are still not equal for men and women. Groups, such as the Liberian Women's Initiative, have fought for women. Government programs have also been set up to help improve women's status in society.

Above: A Liberian woman poses for her wedding photos. According to traditional law, men are allowed to have more than one wife at a time.

Education

Liberian children between ages seven and fifteen must go to school. Students attend elementary school for six years and attend junior high for three years. After junior high school, students take a test. Those who pass the test can go on to senior high school for three years.

During the civil war, many Liberian schools were destroyed. For nearly a decade, most children received little or no education.

Left: Liberian students salute their national flag. A study in 2002 showed that only 40 percent of Liberian children attended school.

Left: These young men once fought in Liberia's civil war, but are now taking a class in woodworking at a vocational school.

Higher Education

There are seven universities in Liberia. Even though all of the universities are independent, they still receive some government money. Liberia also has **vocational** schools, which offer classes in industry, farming, and other subjects.

During the civil war, almost all of Liberia's universities and vocational schools were damaged or destroyed. There are also not enough teachers or supplies. The schools are now using money from international groups to rebuild the schools and restart classes.

Religion

About 40 percent of all Liberians are Christians. Most attend Presbyterian, Lutheran, Roman Catholic, or Baptist churches. Many churches run schools and public programs in Liberia.

About 20 percent of Liberians are Muslims, or followers of the religion of Islam. Like Muslims around the world, they worship in **mosques**, pray five times a day, and observe **Ramadan**.

Below: Liberian Roman Catholics pray during a service at Sacred Heart Cathedral.

In Liberia, the government usually favors the Christian religion. This has made many Liberian Muslims angry and fights between Muslims and the Liberian government have broken out.

Above: Liberians attend a prayer meeting at a Red Cross center for people who lost their homes during the civil war.

Native Religions

About 40 percent of Liberians follow native **animistic** religions. Animistic worship services include lots of singing and dancing. Many Liberians who are Christian or Muslim combine those religions with traditional native beliefs.

Language

Liberia has more than twenty native languages. Liberia's official language, however, is English. Most Liberians speak native languages and English. The English used by the government and taught in schools is American English, but most ordinary Liberians speak Pidgin English. Pidgin English combines the way Liberia's African American founders spoke English in the 1800s with the styles of African languages. In Pidgin English, the word "orange" becomes "orinsh."

Left: A Liberian boy learns how to read and write in English. About 20 percent of Liberians speak only English. Most others can speak English and native Liberian languages.

Left: These shelves display the books of Bernt Karlsson, a Swedish collector of Liberian books.

Literature

Charles E. Cooper, a **diplomat**, wrote Liberia's first novel, *Love in Ebony* (1932). Other important Liberian books include *Murder in the Cassava Patch* (1963) by Bai T. J. Moore and *The Rain and the Night* (1979) by Wilton Sankawulo. Many of Liberia's stories are not in books. Instead, storytellers sing the stories and often dance, too. The folktales they tell help pass on the history and traditions of Liberians.

Arts

Art in Daily Life

In most native Liberian villages, art is a part of daily life. Before the civil war, the Poro and Sande groups taught their members dancing, weaving, sculpture, wood carving, basketry, and music. The groups are not as active as before, but they still teach many traditional arts.

Above: Dawn Padmore is a famous Liberian singer. She left Liberia during the civil war.

Song and Dance

Liberians love to sing. Singing is part of almost any activity in Liberia, from doing household chores to working in the fields or fixing fishnets. Liberians also sing during birth and wedding celebrations and other village events.

Dancing is also an important part of Liberian celebrations. Some Liberian dances are just for men or for women. There is even a dance just for children. One dance of the Dan, or Gio, people is performed by a masked dancer and a drummer. Other dances are performed by many dancers in lines or circles.

Opposite: This young native Liberian dancer poses for a picture in a traditional headdress and white body paint.

Liberian Drums

Drums are important in Liberia. They
are used to keep the beat for musicians,
singers, and dancers. Liberian drums
are played in many ways. Some drums,
such as the *kono* (KOH-noh), are played
with two sticks. Others are hit with
one stick, including the *tardegai* (TAR-
duh-GUY), which is also known as the
damma (DUM-mah). Some drums are
beaten with the player's bare hands,
such as the *djembe* (JEM-bay), which
is also called the *sankpah* (SUNG-pah).

Liberians also play instruments such as the *balafon* (BAH-luh-fawn), a type of xylophone, the *zaza* (ZAH-zah), a kind of shaker, and the *kora* (KOR-rah), a type of stringed instrument.

Liberian Masks

Many Liberian dancers wear wooden masks. Some people believe the masks have religious power. They believe the dancers become the characters or spirits the masks represent. Some masks are used in religious ceremonies. Others are hung on walls to keep evil spirits away.

Above:
This mask was made by the Dan, or Gio, people of northern Liberia. Many traditional masks from Liberia are on display in museums around the world.

Left:
The Dan, or Gio, people are famous for their detailed masks and wood carvings. Many of their wood carvings (*left*) are carved to look like gods or like people.

Leisure

Many Liberians lost their homes and their jobs during the civil war. Today, they must work hard to survive. Most of them have very little time or money for leisure activities. They do spend time with family and friends at festivals and celebrations. These events often include singing and dancing. Liberians also play soccer and board games.

Left: A fisherman moves his boat along a beautiful beach in Singe County. Many Liberian families visit beaches to relax, swim, and have picnics.

Left: These rural Liberian children are playing a ball game. Playing ball games outside is more common in rural villages than in Liberia's cities.

Leisure in Cities and Villages

In the cities, many Liberians spend leisure time dancing in nightclubs. They may also spend time watching television. In the villages, Liberians often watch dancers perform in their village squares. Many rural Liberians also enjoy listening to storytellers.

Throughout Liberia, board games such as *mancala* (mahn-KAH-lah) are popular. The game is also called *kboo* (POOH) and is played by two people.

Soccer in Liberia

Liberians enjoy many sports, but soccer is probably their favorite sport. Liberia has many competitive soccer teams, but lots of Liberians play the sport just for fun. A large number of Liberians also love to watch soccer games.

The top-ranked soccer teams in the country play each other in the National League Championship. The winner of the competition wins Liberia's highest soccer award, the Barclay Shield. The country's national team, the Lone Star, competes against international teams.

Left: This soccer team is traveling to Juazohn, a nearby town, to play in a local soccer match.

Left: George Weah, (*right*) presents the 2001 FIFA World Player of the Year award to Luis Figo (*left*), a player for Spain. In 1995, Weah won the FIFA award and also won player of the year awards for both Africa and Europe.

Liberia's Famous Soccer Players

Many Liberian soccer stars have gone on to play for teams in Europe, in the United States, and in Southeast Asia.

George Weah is probably Liberia's most famous soccer player. He has played for several top teams, including well-known teams in Italy and France. In 1995, Weah won soccer's highest award, the Federation Internationale Football Association (FIFA) World Player of the Year award.

Christian Holidays

Christmas is a major holiday for many Liberian Christians. Most attend special Christmas services. After church, they usually gather to share in a large family meal. Unlike the traditional Christian services of most Americo-Liberians, Christmas services for native Liberians often include lots of African drumming and dancing. In Liberia's rural villages, Christmas services are usually held in the open. The services often include lots of singing and dancing.

Left:
Liberian Catholics attend Palm Sunday services at a church in Monrovia. Most Christian Liberians celebrate the major Christian holidays, such as Good Friday and Easter.

Muslim and Native Festivals

Liberian Muslims celebrate Islamic holidays such as *Eid al-Fitr* (EED al-FIH-tur), a festival that marks the end of Ramadan. Many also celebrate the festival of *Tabaski* (TAH-BAH-skee), which is also called *Eid al-Adha* (EED al-AD-ah). Tabaski honors Abraham's willingness to follow God's orders.

Native Liberian festivals often mark important life events, such as **rites of passage**, weddings, and births. Often, the whole community takes part.

Above:
Liberians celebrate many national holidays, such as Independence Day (July 26), and the birthdays of former presidents Joseph Jenkins Roberts (March 15) and William Tubman (November 29).

Food

Many Liberians love spicy food. They often add black pepper, ginger, and hot peppers to their dishes. Cayenne pepper is especially popular in Liberia.

One of the most common foods in Liberia is cassava. It is often eaten fried or boiled. A thick paste called dumboy is also made from cassava. Pieces of dumboy are usually dipped into a stew or spicy sauce before they are eaten.

Below: A man in Singe County eats dumboy for breakfast.

Left: These women in Grand Bassa County sell palm wine. Palm trees are used to make many things in Liberia, such as palm wine and the red-colored palm oil used to make country chop.

The most common food in Liberia is rice. Rice is most often served with vegetables or a mixture of meat or fish and vegetables. *Jollof* (JAW-lof) is one famous rice dish eaten in Liberia and in other West African nations. Jollof is a mixture of rice, tomatoes, and chicken. In Liberia, pig's feet, bacon, and ham are sometimes added to jollof.

Country chop is another popular dish in Liberia. The dish is made by cooking meat or fish and green vegetables in palm oil. It is usually served over rice.

41

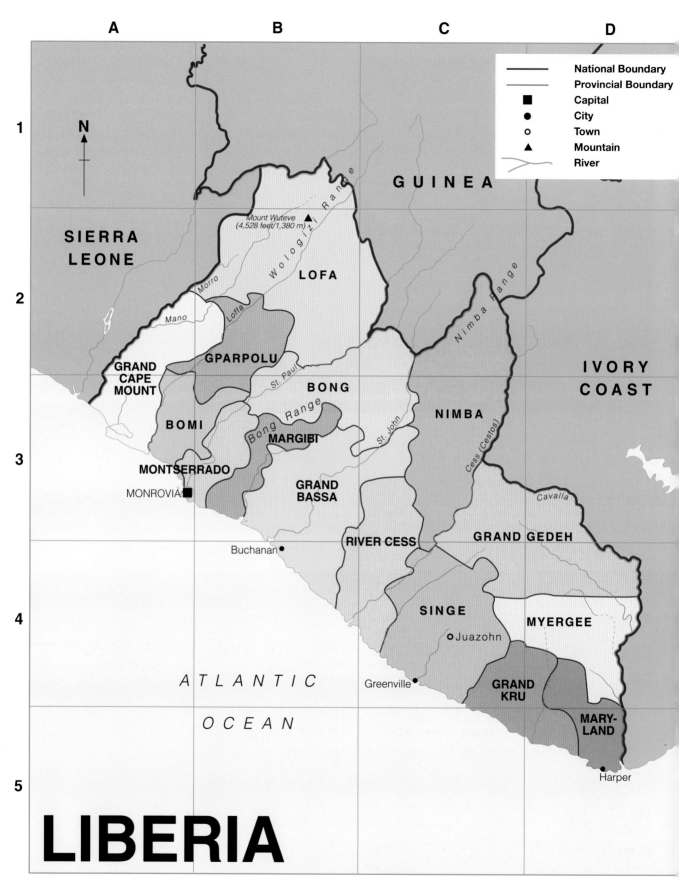

A **B** **C** **D**

1

G U I N E A

**SIERRA
LEONE**

Mount Wuteve
(4,528 feet/1,380 m) ▲

Wologizi Range

LOFA

Morro

2

Mano

Loffa

GPARPOLU

**GRAND
CAPE
MOUNT**

St. Paul

BONG

**IVORY
COAST**

Nimba Range

BOMI

Bong Range

MARGIBI

St. John

NIMBA

Cess (Cestos)

3

MONTSERRADO

MONROVIA ■

**GRAND
BASSA**

Cavalla

RIVER CESS

GRAND GEDEH

Buchanan ●

SINGE

MYERGEE

4

○ Juazohn

A T L A N T I C

Greenville ●

**GRAND
KRU**

**MARY-
LAND**

O C E A N

Harper ●

5

LIBERIA

Above: Liberians use water from rivers for both drinking and bathing.

Atlantic Ocean
A2–D5

Bomi County A2–B3
Bong County B2–C3
Bong Range B3
Buchanan B4

Cavalla River D2–D5
Cess (Cestos) River
B4–D2

Gparpolu County
A2–B3
Grand Bassa
County B3–C3
Grand Cape Mount
County A2–B2
Grand Gedeh
County C3–D4

Grand Kru County
C4–D5
Greenville C4
Guinea A1–D2

Harper D5

Ivory Coast D1–D5

Juazohn C4

Lofa County B1–C2
Loffa River A3–C1

Mano River A2–B1
Margibi County B3
Maryland County
D4–D5
Monrovia A3
Montserrado
County A3–B3
Morro River A3–B2

Mount Wuteve B2
Myergee County
C4–D4

Nimba County
C2–C4
Nimba Range C2

River Cess County
B4–C4

Sierra Leone A1–B2
Singe (Sinoe)
County C4
St. John River
B3–C2
St. Paul River
A3–C2

Wologizi Range
B1–B2

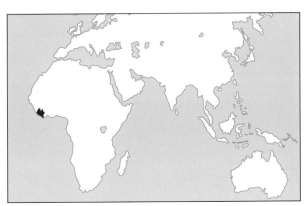

Quick Facts

Official Name   Republic of Liberia

Capital   Monrovia

Official Language   English

Population   3,317,176 (July 2003 estimate)

Land Area   43,000 square miles (111,370 square kilometers)

Counties   Bomi, Bong, Gparpolu (Gparbolu), Grand Bassa, Grand Cape Mount, Grand Gedeh, Grand Kru, Lofa, Margibi, Maryland, Montserrado, Myergee (River Gee), Nimba, River Cess, Singe (Sinoe)

Highest Point   Mount Wuteve (Wutivi) 4,528 feet (1,380 meters)

Major Mountains   Bong Range, Nimba Range, Wologizi Range

Major Rivers   Cavalla, Cess (Cestos), Loffa, Mano, Morro, St. John, St. Paul

Main Religions   native religions, Christianity, Islam

Important Holidays   Birthday of President Joseph Jenkins Roberts (March 15), Unification and Integration Day (May 14), Independence Day (July 26), Flag Day (August 24), Birthday of President William Tubman (November 29)

Currency   Liberian dollar (1 LRD = U.S. $1 in October 2003)

Opposite: Liberians lead a simple life. Tree trunks become a bridge to cross the river.

45

Glossary

animistic: relating to the belief that all things in nature have spirits.

cassava: a root also known as tapioca.

colony: a settlement in one country that is controlled by another country.

constitution: a set of citizen rights and laws for a country's government.

coup: a violent political fight that results in a change of government.

diplomat: a government official who handles relations with other countries.

emblem: a sign or symbol that represents a person, group, or nation.

endangered: are threatened or are in danger of dying out completely.

environmental: relating to nature.

ethnic: related to a race or a culture that has similar customs and languages.

exiled: sent away by force from a person's native land.

export (n): a product sent out of a country to be sold in another country.

inherit: to receive land or valuables after someone, often a family member, dies.

iron ore: natural iron rock before the iron metal has been taken out of it.

lagoons: shallow ponds that connect to larger bodies of water.

mosques: places of worship for people who follow the Islamic religion.

mutiny: a fight against those in control, often aboard a ship.

native: belonging to a land or region by having first grown or been born there.

Ramadan: the Islamic holy month. All healthy Muslims must not eat or drink from dawn to dusk during the month.

rebels: people who fight against a ruler or government.

refugee: relating to people who flee to other countries to escape danger.

republic: a country in which citizens elect their own lawmakers.

rites of passage: ceremonies marking the change from childhood to adulthood.

rural: related to the countryside.

savannas: dry grasslands.

settlement: a small community set up by people from other lands or areas.

urban: related to cities and large towns.

vocational: related to an occupation, profession, or skilled trade.

More Books to Read

A is for Africa. Ifeoma Onyefulu (Puffin)

Head, Body, Legs: A Story from Liberia. Won-Ldy Paye, Margaret H. Lippert (Henry Holt & Company, Inc.)

Koi and the Kola Nuts: A Tale from Liberia. Verna Aardema (Antheneum)

Liberia in Pictures. Visual Geography series. Jo Mary Sullivan, Camille Mirepoix (Lerner Publications)

Liberia. Modern Nations of the World series. Debra A. Miller (Gale Group)

Mommi Watta: Spirit of the River. Virginia Castleman (Flatland Tales)

Mrs. Chicken and the Hungry Crocodile. Won-Ldy Paye, Margaret H. Lippert (Henry Holt & Company, Inc.)

West Africa. Food and Festivals series. Alison Brownlie (Raintree Steck-Vaughn)

Why Leopard Has Spots: Dan Stories from Liberia. Won-Ldy Paye and Margaret H. Lippert (Fulcrum)

Videos

Koi and the Kola Nuts. (Rabbit Ears)

The Village of Round and Square Houses. (Weston Woods)

West Africa. (Elmer Hawkes)

Why Mosquitoes Buzz in People's Ears. (Weston Woods)

Web Sites

cyberschoolbus.un.org/information/index.asp?id=430

en.wikipedia.org/wiki/Liberia

www.worldatlas.com/webimage/countrys/africa/lr.htm

www.kids-online.net/world/liberia.html

Due to the dynamic nature of the Internet, some web sites stay current longer than others. To find additional web sites, use a reliable search engine with one or more of the following keywords to help you locate information about Liberia. Keywords: *Americo-Liberians, Joseph Jenkins Roberts, Mount Wuteve, pygmy hippopotamus.*

Index